From Womb To World

A Mother's Story

Sadaf Steven Lobo

BookLeaf Publishing

India | USA | UK

Dedication

To all the mothers—those waiting to hold their little ones, those embracing the joys and challenges of new motherhood, and those who have walked this path before us.

This book is for the expecting mothers, whose hearts beat in rhythm with the tiny life growing within them, filled with anticipation, love, and endless dreams.

For the new mothers, navigating sleepless nights, first cries, and the overwhelming yet magical transformation of becoming "Mom."

And for all mothers, who give, nurture, and love unconditionally, shaping the world one heartbeat at a time.

May you find comfort, strength, and a reminder that you are never alone in this beautiful, chaotic, and extraordinary journey.

With love and admiration,
Sadaf Lobo

Preface

Motherhood is a journey like no other—one that begins long before a child is born and continues for a lifetime. It is a beautiful paradox of strength and vulnerability, joy and exhaustion, love and sacrifice. From the very first flutter in the womb to the overwhelming love of holding a newborn, every moment changes us in ways we never imagined.

From Womb to World is not just a book; it is a reflection of the emotions, challenges, and triumphs that come with being a mother. Whether you are expecting, navigating the early days of motherhood, or reminiscing about your own journey, this book is for you.

Through personal experiences, shared stories, and heartfelt insights, I hope to offer comfort, encouragement, and a sense of solidarity to every mother who has ever doubted herself, felt overwhelmed, or wondered if she is doing enough. Because the truth is —you are enough.

This book is my tribute to the incredible strength of mothers everywhere. May it remind you that you are never alone in this journey, and that every sleepless

night, every tear wiped away, and every embrace is
shaping a love that is truly unparalleled.

With love and warmth,
Sadaf Lobo

Acknowledgements

This book would not have been possible without the love, support, and inspiration of so many people who have been a part of my journey through motherhood.

First and foremost, I thank my children, who have given me the most profound experience of love, patience, and resilience. You are my greatest teachers, my biggest blessings, and the reason this book exists.

To my husband, for being my rock through the chaos, for holding my hand through the sleepless nights, and for always reminding me that I am doing my best—even when I doubt myself. Your unwavering support means the world to me.

To my parents, who showed me what unconditional love looks like. Your guidance and sacrifices have shaped the mother I am today.

To all the mothers around the world, especially the expecting and new moms—this book is for you. Your strength, love, and dedication deserve to be celebrated every single day.

Lastly, to everyone who encouraged me to put my thoughts into words, who shared their stories, and who reminded me that motherhood is not a solitary journey but a bond that connects us all—thank you.

With all my heart,
Sadaf Lobo

1. The Morning That Changed Everything

I woke to the sun, warm and bright,
A feeling stirred—something felt right.
Days had passed, a month had gone,
A silent question lingered on.

With trembling hands, I took the test,
A tiny hope within my chest.
One line appeared, then came another,
My heart raced—I'm going to be a mother!

I held the strip, my breath so tight,
Ran to my husband, eyes full of light.
His face lit up, his joy unspoken,
A moment pure, a bond unbroken.

With a nervous laugh and a tearful gleam,
I told my mother-in-law—a shared dream.
She blessed me with hands so kind,
Love and happiness intertwined.

Off to work, my heart still soaring,
A secret new, a life restoring.
I dialed my mom, "Ma, guess what?"
Her joy poured through—pure and hot.

And just as joy began to rise,
A wave of nausea took me by surprise.
In the office, I bent, I swayed,
My first vomit—motherhood's first shade.

A day so simple, yet so divine,
A moment where love and fate align.
From that morning, nothing stayed the same,
A tiny heartbeat now knew my name.

2. The Secret Bloomed Within Me

We shared the news, hearts open wide,
With family and friends, beaming with pride.
Their cheers, their joy, their endless delight,
Yet a secret it stayed, hidden from sight.

"For three months, hush," the elders said,
"A fragile time, tread light, not spread."
So we smiled, we glowed, we held it near,
A tiny heartbeat, growing so dear.

Then cravings kicked in—oh, what a treat!
A world of mangoes, juicy and sweet.
Chocolate, ice cream, laddoos too,
Every bite felt fresh and new.

But oh, the office, the endless grind,
A weary body, a restless mind.
Nine to five, no room for rest,
Yet through it all, I did my best.

First-time mom, so much unknown,
How much to pause? How much had grown?
Tired at times, but filled with grace,
A secret life, my heart embraced.

And so the journey had begun,
A path of love, of two made one.

3. A Tiny Dot, A Growing Dream

The joy was pure, the thrill so bright,
Pregnancy felt like love at first sight.
Sleepless nights crept in so slow,
Yet in my heart, a warmth did grow.

No cravings came, but all was fine,
The first trimester passed like time.
Then came the scan, our hearts beat fast,
A tiny dot—our world so vast.

With eager eyes, we sought the sign,
"Is my baby safe? Is all aligned?"
Would it be like Dad or me?
A boy or girl—what will it be?

I checked my belly every day,
Why so small? Is all okay?
A thousand thoughts, a name to find,
Yet love so deep, so undefined.

A guiding hand, a doctor true,
To lead us on as new life grew.
Through every doubt, through every dream,
Our little dot began to gleam.

4. A Mother's Thoughts, A Baby's Dance

The dreams of motherhood took their flight,
A perfect mom—I'd get it right.
With every scan, with every term,
I Googled all, my heart so firm.

Was all okay? Was baby fine?
Each tiny sign, a sacred line.
Then luck arrived, a gift so true,
A job for him, a home brand new.

Second trimester, joys so sweet,
A growing bond, a rhythmic beat.
A movie night, a world so loud,
And baby kicked—so strong, so proud.

With every thump, a story spun,
A life within, our hearts as one.
Through every sound, through every move,
Our love just grew—a perfect groove.

5. A Silent Storm

The days feel heavy, the nights so long,
A silent storm, yet I smile so strong.
Tears stand ready, but I push them away,
Because I must smile, come what may.

Lonely whispers echo inside,
No one to hear, no place to hide.
I reach for him, but he's far in the day,
Work and duty pull him away.

Small things sting, they cut so deep,
Anxiety wakes when I try to sleep.
I hold my breath, I hold my ground,
Yet no one sees, no one hears a sound.

But I am more than these weary sighs,
More than the weight behind my eyes.
I carry life, I carry love,
A heart so strong, it rises above.

So I'll breathe, I'll rest, I'll take my time,
This storm will pass, the sun will shine.
And though it feels like I'm alone,
I know my strength, I've always known.

6. I Remember

I was told to eat, but only what's right,
Not what I craved in the dead of night.
I was told to work, to keep moving on,
No time to rest, though my strength was gone.

I was told to sleep less, though I was drained,
My body aching, my soul restrained.
And when I spoke of the pain inside,
They shrugged it off, no arms open wide.

"Everyone goes through this," they'd say,
As if my struggles should fade away.
No warmth, no comfort, just empty lines,
As I sat alone with racing minds.

Husband and mother-in-law busy each day,
And I, in silence, drifted away.
Creeping thoughts, shadows so deep,
Was this only my child to keep?

Yet through the loneliness, through the ache,
A tiny heartbeat for whom I wake.
And though the world may turn aside,
I'll hold my baby, full of pride.

7. A Baby Shower to Remember

The room was bright, the air was light,
A day of joy, a heart's delight.
With laughter ringing, love so true,
A precious time for me and you.

The guessing game, a moment sweet,
He chose a girl—his heart's own beat.
Smiles and cheers, a love-filled space,
Tears of joy streamed down my face.

One aunt draped my saree tight,
Another adorned my hair just right.
Hands so warm, hearts so near,
Wrapped in love, I held back tears.

Gifts and blessings, memories made,
A day of magic, a bond displayed.
A moment cherished, forever mine,
A shower of love, pure and divine.

8. Cravings, Questions & Tiny Kicks

I craved for sweets, an endless spree,
Mangoes danced like dreams in me.
But joy turned sharp, like needles' bite,
An itch that stole my sleep at night.

A mystery meal, what had I eaten?
My calm was lost, my peace was beaten.
The time drew near, the clock ran fast,
And fears began to gather, vast.

Will I be strong? Will I survive?
Will pain consume or keep me alive?
Normal birth or a C-section way?
Will I make it to see the day?

If I don't, who'll hold my child tight,
Sing lullabies and kiss goodnight?
Who'll know her smile, her little frown,
Who'll turn her world around?

In the hush of scans, I saw a sign—
Tiny hands and feet in line.
A flicker, a kick, a twist, a wave,
A love so deep, so pure, so brave.

Despite the fear, I held on tight,
For you, my baby, my heart's own light.
A storm of thoughts, yet love was loud—
My soul, my strength, my silent vow.

9. Ready for the Day, Not for the Nights

I stretched and breathed, I bent with grace,
Did yoga flows at my own pace.
Housework done, steps on repeat,
Dreaming of labor strong and sweet.

YouTube guided, pose by pose,
For normal birth — that's how it goes.
The hospital bag was packed with care,
Diapers, blankets, slippers — all were there.

I thought I knew what lay ahead,
The birth, the push, the tears I'd shed.
But no one said what follows through,
The silent storm that motherhood knew.

The sleepless nights, the aching cry,
The need for help, no one nearby.
Prepared I was — or so I thought,
But some truths living alone had taught.

Not every lesson books will show,
Some things only new moms know.
Still, through it all, I find my way,
With love that grows more every day.

10. A Silent Hero — My Mother

In the stillness of my chaos, you were always near,
A gentle voice, a source of cheer.
Though miles apart, you felt so close,
In your quiet strength, my courage rose.

Through sleepless nights and weary days,
You guided me in countless ways.
Not with loud words, but love so deep,
You held me up when I couldn't sleep.

A call away, just one soft tone,
And I no longer felt alone.
Your wisdom calmed my every storm,
In your warmth, my world was warm.

Like a pillar, strong and ever true,
I stood because I leaned on you.
You gave me strength, you gave me grace,
In every trial, you held your place.

God knew His reach would need another,
So in His love, He made a mother.
And in His wisdom, He gave me you—
My silent hero, forever true.

11. In His Arms , I Broke

I went for a checkup, just routine, they said,
Near the due date, thoughts gently led.
But a sudden pain, a shift so slight,
The doctor's words changed day to night.

"You're dilating now, it won't be long,"
My heart beat fast, yet I had to be strong.
With my mother and MIL right by my side,
Their calm presence stemmed the tide.

A call to my love, "Come, it's time,"
He left from work, rushed through the grime.
But oh, the PV—the dreaded test,
I cried in pain, there was no rest.

They gave the gel, the needle, the fear,
Each hour passed, the pain drew near.
By nightfall, labor's storm had begun,
I was scared, I prayed, I wished to run.

Then he arrived—my anchor, my shore,
I broke in his arms, couldn't take it anymore.
Tears streamed down, I clung so tight,
Wishing this darkness would bring me light.

Each contraction, a wave, each breath, a fight,
But I held onto love through that endless night.
And though I trembled, tired and sore—
I was becoming a mother... nothing mattered more.

12. A Scar Called Love

My grandma came, her smile so wide,
Excitement twinkling in her eyes with pride.
The night grew long, yet none felt still,
Doctors and nurses, in and out at will.

The contractions hit like crashing waves,
No sleep, just strength my body gave.
Each minute passed, a test of grace,
Pain etched deep across my face.

At 5 a.m., the silence broke—
A monitor's beep, a worried stroke.
"The heartbeat's dropping," the doctor said,
A sudden chill, a wave of dread.

Urgency rang through every hall,
A choice, a signature—no time to stall.
To the OT, I was swiftly wheeled,
My heart raced faster than it could feel.

Anaesthesia crept like a silent tide,
My limbs went cold, my breath had cried.
I heard the words, "We're starting now,"
Fear clenched tight—I furrowed my brow.

A cut, a tug, then moments blur—
And then I heard the tiniest stir.
"It's a girl!" the doctor beamed,
My soul lit up, I almost dreamed.

Tears welled up, a silent prayer,
Thank You, God, for this love so rare.
I drifted off in peaceful sweep,
As stitches closed what pain made deep.

That's the night my life transformed,
With scars of strength, a heart reborn.
A warrior's birth, not less, not wrong—
That's how I became a C-section mom.

13. The Morning She Arrived

On June 11th, 2022, the morning light,
Brought with it joy, pure and bright.
A baby girl, our precious one,
Our hearts lit up like the rising sun.

Still numb with the drugs, yet full of grace,
I opened my eyes and saw her face.
All the pain just slipped away,
As love and peace chose to stay.

My husband's joy, too vast to hide,
He held my hand and stayed by my side.
In every moment, through every tear,
His strength and love kept me near.

Four soft days in a healing cocoon,
Wrapped in warmth, morning and moon.
Then home we went, with hearts so wide,
Where love and blessings did abide.

My mother-in-law stood by the door,
Holy water sprinkled on the floor.
A sweet welcome, so full of grace,
Joy and tradition in every embrace.

Yet one face missed in the light that day,
A silent wish, a soft ache that stays.
My father-in-law, gone, but near—
In every tear, in every cheer.

Family, friends, came pouring in,
With happy hearts and wide-eyed grins.
"Does she look like her dad? Or maybe you?"
Their words were tender, their joy so true.

She was the answer to every prayer,
A blessing beyond all we could bear.
Our lives were changed, our hearts were won—
With the light of our little one.

14. Between Love and Fear

A japa maid, with caring hands,
Came each day, as love commands—
To soothe my body, calm my soul,
And bathe my baby, make us whole.

For one and a half months, side by side,
She helped me heal with every stride.
Six months of leave, I had in grace,
To live this dream, to feel her face.

My precious girl, my world so new,
A love so pure, so deep, so true.
Like every mom, I smiled and wept,
While rocking her as she softly slept.

But soon, the joy turned into haze,
The nights grew long, the darkest phase.
Loneliness crept, so soft, so slow,
I lost my calm, let patience go.

Anxiety whispered fears at night,
"What if she's gone out of my sight?"
"What if I vanish, fade away?
Who'll love her like I do each day?"

Bad dreams came and wouldn't leave,
My heart began to silently grieve.
I didn't know, I couldn't see—
Postpartum shadows haunting me.

But through the fear, and all that pain,
I found the strength to smile again.
Because even in the darkest part,
A mother holds the brightest heart.

15. A Working Mom's Heart

So here it comes, the end of leave,
With trembling heart, I had to grieve.
To part from her, my tiny light,
For dreams ahead, I chose the fight.

I kissed her cheek, then turned away,
A silent tear marked start of day.
My soul felt heavy, time moved slow,
While thoughts of her refused to go.

The clock hands dragged, I watched them crawl,
Her giggles echoed through it all.
And when it struck that hour of seven,
I raced back home — my slice of heaven.

It's never easy, not at all,
To rise each time you start to fall.
A mother breaks in silent ways,
Then builds her world with love each day.

She trades her dreams, her quiet nights,
Her books, her songs, her carefree flights.
Her world now spins on lullaby tunes,
Messy buns and afternoon noons.

In husband's tee and faded pants,
She dances still, though not by chance.
She lives for smiles and tiny hugs,
For "Mama" calls and bedtime tugs.

No jewels, no praise, no perfect plan,
She only wants what love she can.
A warm embrace, a word, a smile,
To feel it's all been so worthwhile.

So if you see her tired and worn,
Know she's the reason hearts are born.
And in her quiet strength you'll see,
She flips the world — for family.

16. Postpartum Echoes

As motherhood began, my world rearranged,
Sleepless nights and love — everything changed.
I learned it's not easy, not simple or sweet,
With joy in my arms and pain at my feet.

My mother-in-law — a blessing, it's true,
Retired her dreams so I could pursue.
She held the baby, gave all that she had,
Even when moments turned heavy or sad.

There were days of silence, of words left unsaid,
Of things that were spoken that rang in my head.
Like, "I did this for my son, so must we..."
But why can't my children grow differently?

I was new, still learning, finding my way,
Just needed a hug, not advice every day.
I wanted a whisper: "You're doing just fine,"
Not judgment disguised in a passive design.

"You chose the easy way," they'd say with a sigh,
As if slicing me open was easy to try.
They doubted the doctor, the monitors' sound,
While I lay there praying my baby's still around.

The heartbeat was dropping — I saw the fear,
But they weren't there, they weren't near.
And when they said, "They do it for pay,"
I quietly broke a little that day.

Postpartum came, a quiet storm,
Not always in tears, but far from the norm.
I craved a soft voice to say, "You are strong,"
Instead I was told that my choices were wrong.

And though time moves on, healing the skin,
The echoes of those days live deep within.
A postpartum mother remembers it all —
The rise, the stumble, the climb, the fall.

The good, the bad, the happy, the pain,
The lonely night feeds, the tears in the rain.
We carry the weight, but still, we stand tall,
Because motherhood asks everything — and we give it
all.

17. A Birthday of Blessings

As time flew by on wings so light,
Her first birthday came, pure and bright.
No grand affair, no lavish scene,
Just something simple, pure, serene.

We made a plan, a thoughtful one,
To spread some joy, to share the sun.
With children dressed in humble grace,
At a convent — a sacred place.

We brought them books, and uniforms too,
For blessings strong, for skies so blue.
In return, we asked no gold,
Just love for her — a heart to hold.

My tiny tot, in yellow dressed,
A silver crown upon her crest.
She giggled, played with every child,
Their laughter ringing free and wild.

The cake was cut with hands so small,
And shared with joy among them all.
They clapped and sang, "Happy Birthday dear!"
Their voices sweet, sincere, and clear.

No guests, no gifts, no party loud,
Just quiet hearts and spirits proud.
A day of love, so purely spun,
Wrapped in grace from everyone.

For blessings bloom in giving hands,
More than gifts or grander plans.
And that's how we chose her day to be —
A memory etched in humility.

18. My Samaira , My Heart

You've changed me in ways I never knew,
A world once grey, now bathed in hue.
You're my sunshine, my morning light,
My joy, my laughter, my sweetest sight.

When you say "Mumma," my soul takes flight,
I'd give you my heart without a fight.
Your voice, so soft, a melody so sweet,
With every word, my world feels complete.

Your care, your love, so pure, so true,
In your little ways, you always knew
How to heal, how to make me smile,
How to make each moment worthwhile.

You love your Dadda a little more—
But Samaira, in my heart, you roar.
You're my heartbeat, my every breath,
My forever love, in life and death.

I can't imagine a day, not one,
Without you in it, my precious one.
You're a beautiful soul, a gift divine,
Forever and always, you'll be mine.

The love I feel, no words can trace,
No one, nothing, could take your place.
When you're hurt, my heart breaks too,
I'd bear your pain to comfort you.

And though you're just three, still small and bright,
The thought of your future keeps me up at night.
One day you'll marry, start life anew—
But oh, my Samaira, I'll always miss you.

You're not going anywhere, not from me,
You're my daughter, my soul, my destiny.
A love like this, no time can sever,
You're mine, my angel, now and forever.

19. Grateful Heart, Full of Love

This journey of motherhood, wild and new,
I've walked with strength—but not alone, it's true.
Behind each smile, each sleepless night,
Were hearts that held me, shared the fight.

To my husband, my anchor, steady and kind,
Your love and patience ease my mind.
Through tired eyes and tiny cries,
You've been my calm, my lullabies.

To my mother-in-law, with your gentle care,
Your wisdom flows through every prayer.
You've stood by me with love so deep,
Rocked my babies, let me sleep.

To my parents, my guiding light,
Your endless support has felt so right.
From childhood days to being a mom,
You've been my courage, kept me calm.

To my sister, my soul, my forever friend,
Your love and help, there's no end.
In laughter, tears, and little mess,
You've shared it all—more, never less.

And to all the hearts who've been there too,
Who offered help and saw me through—
The hands that held, the words that cheered,
The love that wiped away each fear.

I thank you all, from deep inside,
With love and pride I cannot hide.
Motherhood's path is not just mine—
It's built by those who helped me shine.

20. To My Sweet Little Girl

Tiny hands, a heart so pure,
A laughter that makes life feel sure,
Your smile is the sun that lights my day,
In your embrace, all fears fade away.

With every step, you teach me how
To love so deeply, here and now.
A world of wonder in your eyes,
Where every dream can touch the skies.

You dance in joy, without a care,
And leave a trail of magic there.
With every word, each tender sound,
You make our love the strongest bound.

So, little one, as you grow and play,
Know that my love will never stray.
You're the rhythm in my heart's beat,
The reason my world feels complete.

Forever yours, in every way,
Your love is my guide, come what may.

38

21. To All the Moms – I See You

This is for all the moms, doing an amazing job,
Silently strong, through every tear and sob.
Each journey is different, each path uniquely tough,
And sometimes, even love around doesn't feel enough.

The ones closest may not always see,
The weight you carry, silently.
There are moments you're shattered, torn apart,
But one look at your child, and you restart.

Motherhood—it's a thankless role,
No rewards, no titles, no payroll.
No "promotion" for the sleepless nights,
Just tiny hands that make it right.

They say parents share the load—
But we know, moms walk the heaviest road.
It's 90% us, with hearts on fire,
Juggling roles, drained but never tired.

We're daughters, wives, sisters too,
Each role demanding, without a clue
That we're breaking inside, still wearing a smile,
Going that extra, thankless mile.

While the world sleeps in peaceful grace,
A mom's mind runs a midnight race.
Thoughts swirling, worries deep—
But still, she hushes her child to sleep.

Yet we rise, every single day,
Gathering our broken pieces on the way.
Because our children need us strong and whole,
So we patch up pain and play our role.

To all the women who've felt this deep,
Your strength is quiet, your love runs steep.
I salute you, queens, for all you do,
This world would break without women like you.

Thank you for reading, for feeling each line,
For giving my journey a moment of your time.
Part 2 is coming, so stay near—
More love, more truth, more strength to cheer.

www.ingramcontent.com/pod-product-compliance
Lightning Source LLC
LaVergne TN
LVHW041241200726
843507LV00013B/2762